ABOUT THE AUTHOR

EUNICE OLUMIDE is a supermodel, activist and curator. Born in Edinburgh to Nigerian parents, she has appeared in both national and international fashion campaigns, working for top couture houses such as Christopher Kane, Alexander McQueen and Mulberry. A committed philanthropist, she works closely with a number of charities including CHAS, The Well Foundation, Zero Waste Scotland and Best Beginnings, and is a patron for Adopt an Intern. Eunice was awarded an MBE in the 2017 Birthday Honours list for services to arts and media, and was appointed Design Champion by The Victoria and Albert Museum in Dundee in 2018.

HOW TO GET INTO FASHION

A complete guide for models, creatives and anyone interested in the world of fashion

EUNICE OLUMIDE

Luath Press Limited
EDINBURGH
www.luath.co.uk

First published 2018

ISBN: 978-1-912147-73-1 HBK
ISBN: 978-1-912147-72-4 PBK

The paper used in this book is recyclable. It is made from
low chlorine pulps produced in a low energy, low emissions
manner from renewable forests.

Printed and bound by
Martins the Printer, Berwick upon Tweed

Typeset in 11 point Sabon by 3btype.com

Photographs reproduced with kind permission of the
photographers detailed in the photograph credits section
at the end of the book.

*For all those who were
mistreated along the way*

Contents

Acknowledgements

I'd like to say a special thank you to all the wonderful people who helped make this book possible: British fashion commentator and Professor of Diversity, Caryn Franklin; supermodel Richard Biedul; author and journalist Lucy Siegle; fashion director at Rankin's *Hunger* magazine, Kim Howells; Susan Angoy; Doug Wood; special thank you to the prolific artist Bradley Theodore, for the cover image; and photographers Maximilian Hetherington, Ioannis Koussertari, Dawn Marie Jones, Arved Colvin-Smith, William Pine and Morgan White. And especially to my mother, Victoria Edwards, for always being so supportive throughout my career and my life. Thanks mum.

Introduction

WHEN I ORIGINALLY came up with the idea for this book it was to answer the many requests from friends, clients and fans who would all ask me the same question: 'How do I get into fashion?' Having experienced the industry first hand, I lost count of the people who gave me completely contradictory advice. And because there are virtually no manuals or guides out there to offer any kind of sensible, practical help, it became more and more obvious to me over time that much of this advice would send people in completely the wrong direction. In the very worst cases, I came across models who had been badly treated simply because they were unsure about the boundaries of the occupation, what they might be asked to do and how their image could be misused or even exploited. So my primary concern is to protect people from putting themselves in situations that are not productive or necessary to achieve their dreams. I hope you'll enjoy reading my book.

To give you a little bit of background, I was born in Edinburgh, Scotland and was originally scouted at the age of 15 by one of London's top model agencies. Back then, I knew next to nothing about the fashion industry and had absolutely no desire to be involved in it. But, after being scouted a further four times, I eventually decided to give it a go and see where it could take me. Amazingly, it turned out to become my lifelong career and, as one of Scotland's first black models, I worked in the UK, the United States of America, Japan, France, Italy, Spain, Germany and the United Arab Emirates. I was signed to top modelling agencies AMQ, The Model Team, Colours, IMM Dusseldorf, Nemesis and Viva & LAAgencia. I've appeared in both national and international advertising campaigns, fashion weeks and editorials such as *WAD*, *ID*, *News Week*, *Hello*, *OK*, *ES Magazine*, *Stylist*, *Dazed & Confused*, *Oyster*, *Paper Cut*, *New York Magazine*, *Vogue*, *Vogue Italia*, *Bahrain Confidential*, *London Fashion Week Daily*, *Harper's Bazaar*, *Luire*, *Tatler*, *Hunger* and many more. And at the grand old age of 27, I began to be talked about as a supermodel. Walking the runway was always my favourite place to be and I loved modelling for the likes of Mulberry, Alexander McQueen, Christopher Kane, Swarovski, Alexander Wang and Harris Tweed as well as fronting campaigns for brand giants such as The Body Shop.

In 2017 I was honoured by Her Majesty the Queen for my services to arts and media and received an MBE, alongside fellow supermodel Erin O'Connor, author

JK Rowling and musician Ed Sheeran. So, eventually, I achieved my dream of not only becoming highly successful within the fashion industry but also being able to contribute something towards the greater fashion world and being recognised for it in a way that exceeded even my own expectations.

Although it's been hard work, I've had a fabulous time during my modelling career and I was brought up by my mum to be supremely grateful to the universe for every opportunity that came my way.

But, as well as enjoying the glitz and the glamour, I've also felt I should use my profile to draw attention to and raise awareness for a number of charities that are dear to my heart. These include CHAS, The Well Foundation, Zero Waste Scotland, Love Music Hate Racism, Best Beginnings and St Columba's Hospice. In 2013, I was asked to be an ambassador for the Fashion Targets Breast Cancer Campaign, joining individuals such as Kate Moss, Edith Bowman, Twiggy, Alan Carr and Sharon & Kelly Osborne, and became a patron for Adopt an Intern. And in 2018, the V&A in Dundee appointed me as Design Champion.

CHAPTER ONE

How to Be Successful

WELL DONE, you have just taken the first step towards living the life and achieving the career that you really want. And now, it's my mission to demystify the fashion industry for you and show you how to plot a clear route to achieving your goal.

You may have bought this book because you know exactly what it is that you want to do. Or it might be because you're not quite sure yet. Whatever the reason, when you've finished reading you'll have a much better understanding of the industry and be able to decide if fashion really is for you. You'll also have a healthier perspective on the various career paths that are available to you. One thing is certain though: behind everything we want to achieve, I'm convinced there lies a deeper connection to our subconscious, how we really feel about ourselves and where we are at this specific moment in time. I've learnt a lot of lessons in my life and one of the most important ones is that if you don't believe in yourself and think you deserve to be successful, it's highly unlikely that anyone else will believe in you either.

A lack of self-belief is the main reason why so many people fail to achieve their dreams. You must trust that your dreams are completely attainable and that you deserve them to come true. This comes from a place of love. Loving yourself will make you capable of being the best you can be, and it will also give you the strength you need to survive when others do not support you. Above all, it will make you more attractive to the rest of the world. Other key qualities you must try to develop to be successful are patience, perseverance and resilience. Define what success means to you and, rather than judging your progress by how someone else is doing, judge it on the goals that you have set for yourself and how far you've gone towards achieving them. We're all born with different life chances, which are often beyond our control. For instance, you may have grown up with everything you need in life or you may have had very little. Loving yourself is the start of making your life the way you want it to be. Loving everything and everyone else around you will bring peace and happiness.

On the same basis, the people you associate with, the places you go to and where you spend most of your time will influence how successful you will be. You must believe that you deserve the best in life. If you don't, and when opportunities come knocking, you may allow them to pass you by. Another important thing in life is preparation. What I mean by that is if you want to work in fashion or any other industry, you must do everything you can to ensure that when the opportunity arises you are ready to capitalise on it. If you're not ready, you may find yourself in a life changing position that you are unable to take advantage of because you weren't ready for it. This could be something as simple as always having a pack of business cards handy to give out to people who could be of help to you.

Love is at the heart of our progress as human beings. If you allow jealously or hatred to become part of your consciousness, it will impede your progress. You will never be able to be the best you can be. This may mean changing your environment, allowing new people and friends to come into your life and, most importantly, changing your mentality. Look at it this way: if your life is disorganised and your friends and the people you surround yourself with are dysfunctional, it will be very difficult for you to flourish. Of course, you may have good reason for not liking someone but ultimately killing them with kindness and your success is the best remedy for dealing with those who don't believe in you. It will liberate you and it will allow you to win at everything you put your mind to. You must want to be the best.

When people are negative towards you or your dream, understand that this often comes from their own lack of ability to believe in themselves. Their judgement and treatment of you and others can be stark because when you don't follow your dreams you can become bitter. Think about it: if you meet a couple who are truly in love they will also want everyone else around them to be happy. No matter what path you choose or what career you go into, you mustn't fear being alone. If you're at peace and happy with yourself, you will attract other people who are also happy and at peace with themselves. These are the people who will help and support you to be the best you can be. And whenever you feel sad or down, remember this: there are millions of people on this planet who don't even have food with which to feed themselves or their family. Use this to motivate yourself to do better. If we cannot help others, the least we can do is to be grateful for what we have and remember that no matter how difficult your life might be, there are always many more people in the world who have nothing in comparison to you.

Never allow your own ego or pride to stop you from achieving your dreams. Be humble, understanding, and sympathetic and most importantly be grateful for every opportunity that is given to you. When you are truly content and happy for what you have, you will automatically attract positivity into your own life. Look at and study the lives of people you see who are successful. The odds are that this didn't happen by chance and, in the majority of cases, you'll find the most successful people can also be the most approachable.

Remember: you are the master of your life and you alone control where you go, who you see, how you are seen, how you live and how you dress. So surround yourself with like-minded people. This will set you on the right road to acquire the life and career that you really want. Don't be afraid to travel; it may be the case that where you live now will provide you with fewer opportunities. Never deny your talent and your worth. You are a powerful human being and one person can change and impact the world. You can achieve your dream. And, like me, you may even find yourself going above and beyond what you could have ever imagined.

This book is not only for those who want to get into the fashion industry but to encourage self-belief and the importance of being humble, kind and loving to everything and everyone. When you do make it, never be selfish. Remember those who have helped and inspired you on the way and seek to help and motivate others in any way you can.

Fashion Realities

The fashion industry has long been branded as the originator of body hate or dysmorphia. But in reality, it's not to anyone's benefit to have young men or women worrying about their weight. I have identified some specific guidelines on 'body types' later in chapter two and, when you understand them, you'll be able to identify your own unique look and determine which areas of modelling you're best suited.

One of the most common questions I get asked is: 'How do you go about finding an agent?' Of course, anyone can go online and gather some names and addresses of model agencies to write to. But if you don't understand how to present yourself properly, or even how to choose the correct images to send, your application may not even make it past the receptionist. As in many areas of life, things that seem obvious to one person may not be quite so clear to others. And in a lot of ways, it's this ambiguity that protects the exclusivity of the industry itself. The purpose here is to help you prepare yourself and understand where you fit in. This will then enable you to approach the right agency or create the best strategy to achieve a successful career.

Unlike other industries, access to real professional advice can be limited and formal training only comes when you are actually signed to a model agency. This book details not only where to start and how to become a model, but most importantly what other roles are available within the industry. The process of creating, buying and selling clothes means that fashion has many associated occupations. They include everything from fashion buying to public relations and styling to photography. I'll describe these different types of opportunities in detail for you later so you can get a better idea of the full scope available.

In many ways, being a fashion model can be compared to the life of a professional footballer. You might get signed, but the work doesn't stop there. In fact, it's only just begun. You'll be transferred and trialled in other countries and possibly make the annual pilgrimage from London to New York. In many cases, you will be paid according to your equity, which is defined by how established you are or what previous campaign work you might have done. You must then be booked continuously for the right campaigns and catwalk events to have any sort of a career. Nothing is guaranteed, and nothing is definite. At any given moment, trends in the market place can change like the weather and you will often, as in the case of football or other creative industries, not necessarily make a real living wage until you are able to secure the appropriate bookings.

You may also accrue an assortment of financial costs depending on how the agency you're signed to works. It's imperative that you understand how the industry operates internally, in order to give yourself the very best chance of becoming successful. This book gives clear guidance on how to build a portfolio, cultivate the correct attitude, look after your health and nutrition, and deal with rejection. Take the time to read the information and contacts at the end of this book – it's all useful stuff and good to know. It's all here. So not only will you be prepared for what is truly expected of you both physically and mentally, you can make sure that you don't put yourself in a position to be exploited.

CHAPTER TWO

How to Identify Your Look

MOST PEOPLE DON'T realise that there is a variety of different model types within the fashion industry. It is vital you identify your own 'look' early on as this will help you save invaluable time and money.

The body types shown below tend to be a good indicator of the modelling category that may suit you best:

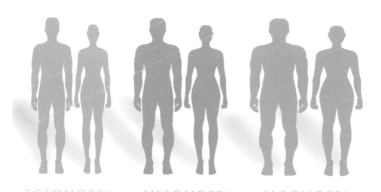

ECTOMORPH   MESOMORPH   ENDOMORPH

Editorial High Fashion

The first body type is called ectomorph or, for our purposes, an editorial body shape. This look is the one that most people aspire to and tends to receive the most publicity. Editorial means that you are suitable for high fashion. It will include top fashion labels such as Chanel, Dolce & Gabbana, Vivienne Westwood, Bulgari, Alexander McQueen and iconic magazines like *Vogue*, *V* and *Pop*. Editorial models with a high fashion look include Alek Wek, Kate Moss, Cara Delevigne, Adwoa Aboah and Naomi Campbell. If you have the right height as well as the right look, you can also find yourself being cast for fashion shows.

It's a common myth that fashion shows are where someone takes garments off a hanger from the shop floor and simply throws them onto a model, who then appears from behind a curtain and struts down a runway posing for the audience. You've got to remember that a fashion show is a massive opportunity for a designer to showcase his or her collection, not only to industry professionals, but also to the world's press and buyers from retail stores and boutiques. The media will publish images from the show and these will then help to spread the word about the new never-before-seen work of the designer. Buyers are the people who come looking for new fashions for the season. They will then select the best garments for their shops (I go into more detail on this subject later in the book).

Female models that do high fashion tend to be around a 24–25inch waist. Now, obviously, this is an area that has caused huge controversy within the industry with much concern being generated around the impact on the models' health. Perhaps this is to do with what is referred to as 'sample size'. This is this consistent, standard small size most designers create their couture pieces to for catwalk shows. It is most likely more cost effective and means, regardless of which countries they are showing their collection in, all the models will fit the same garment, hence the name 'sample size'. However, there is some good news, the industry is finally starting to change its attitudes – albeit slowly. But there's still a long way to go. As a general rule of thumb, female catwalk models have to be no shorter than 5ft9, and men between 5ft11 and 6ft2.

Although high fashion models have the opportunity to be cast for the top fashion couture houses, it can be harder to make a real living wage. This is because there are fewer paid jobs. In fact, it's something of a fable that all runway models make a lot of money. In some very rare cases, it is possible to earn a high salary, but for most, the money can be quite poor. In fact, models who do commercial work tend to have a more stable or sustainable income compared to fashion models. If you become 'established' you are more than likely to have a great career in front of you. This means that you have successfully secured several national or international campaigns. In other words, you have been chosen to become the face of a company or a brand.

Commercial Advertising

This area of modelling is generally referred to within the industry as commercial and means that the way you look has a more general appeal to the audience which can be used to enhance or to define a company's image. This may include companies on the high street such as JD Sports, Boohoo, ASOS, Mountain Range, Footlocker, Sainsbury's, HMV, Boots, House of Fraser and popular magazines such as *Good Housekeeping*. So your look should be one that appeals to the everyday consumer; someone that people feel they can identify with. They should be able to easily imagine themselves looking like you and using the products that you are selling. This part of the industry tends to be the most ethnically diverse and usually the models must be more traditionally beautiful. You might be thinking: 'But aren't all models beautiful?' And the answer to that is yes, the same way that all people are incredible in their own way. But what we mean here is that their beauty is more 'obvious'. To understand this further think about the way that a pageant queen looks, such as Miss World, and then apply that criteria to various body types, ethnicities and shapes.

As a commercial model you could be shooting advertisements and catalogues for swimwear, lingerie, hair and bridal wear. So, ultimately you'll have a much more regular supply of jobs since most people use these products and brands more regularly. Models that shoot commercial and lifestyle work can be ectomorph, mesomorph or endomorphs – any body size in fact. This is because when the consumer browses through their catalogues and magazines, they want to see someone who looks like they would use that tennis racket, gardening equipment or washing detergent. The types of modelling I'm talking about here can vary considerably but usually include the following:

Ambassadors and Spokes-models

These models tend to live a lifestyle that is synonymous with that of the particular brand. For instance, you may become an ambassador because you have something in common with the company, ie a sports brand may contract a top athlete to do modelling for them.

Promotional Models

In this area of the industry models are often booked to work at trade shows such as ExCel London or in shopping centres up and down the country. You may not be shooting any pictures at all; instead your role may be to serve, look after guests or simply to draw attention and inform the customer about a product. Promotional models are usually encouraged to have a bright and engaging personality and a ready smile.

Print Models

These models will largely be shot for advertising campaigns and magazines, so height isn't particularly important – they vary in height and be as short as 5ft6.

Alternative Modelling

If you have a truly inspiring look, or there's something that separates you from the rest, this type of modelling may be best for you. Such models can have extensive piercings or tattoos or distinctive dental work. There is a major market for alternative models and jobs can range from editorials to trade shows.

Sports Models

You don't have to be a professional athlete to model sports gear, but it's really important that you're fit and in great physical shape. Shoots will mostly be for big sports related brands, obviously, and sometimes companies might want to promote a dynamic sporty image in their advertising – yoghurts and other healthy foods spring to mind – so there's quite a lot of scope for this kind of modelling work.

Plus Size Models

Contrary to popular belief, if you fall into this category – a full figure and size 14 to 16 plus – you may have the opportunity to work in both commercial and high fashion. Top model Ashley Graham from the United States is a prime example.

As a model of any kind, you may be asked to do bikini, lingerie, partially nude, nude or implied nude work. You must decide if you're comfortable with that. True, there are some models who can avoid this due to their charismatic personality and professional dedication. But think very carefully, as many new faces won't be quite so discerning. Ultimately, if you're not at ease with nudity, you may want to let your booker and agency know in advance. That way they won't put you up for those kinds of jobs. The downside is that you may earn yourself a reputation for being difficult to work with and you might not get the jobs you want. This is unfortunate and, in some cases, even unfair. However, it's still entirely possible to have a career without accepting every single job that your agent or client asks you to do. When all's said and done, it's your life and you must make the right choices for you.

Happily, there are many different body types and modelling opportunities within the industry. In fact, you can make a good living without setting one foot on the catwalk – whatever size or body shape you are. You must identify your look and use that to work out where you will operate at your highest capacity. Never compromise your integrity or do anything that is against how you really feel inside. Only you should define and create your path.

An incredible visionary, supporter and matriarch within fashion was Editor of *Vogue Italia*, Franca Sozzani. She stressed that the key to becoming a successful model is to have will power and personality. It will be these parts of you that will make you stand out from the crowd.[1]

CHAPTER THREE

How to Get an Agent

TO WORK IN fashion, you must be confident. Please note that this doesn't mean you should be arrogant. That kind of behaviour is not encouraged and may just lose you the very opportunity you're looking for. Remember: less is more. Try to focus, remain calm, still and quiet. That way, you allow the person who is assessing you to consider your potential.

Also, it is extremely important to show your natural beauty so do not go in to see an agent with a face full of make-up, hair extensions or any other enhancements. Instead, opt for very minimal or no make-up at all. And if you've got long hair, tie it back so that people can see your face.

Polaroids

Get a friend or a family member to take some photos of you. They don't need to be professional. Agents just want to see 'the real you' and they're more than capable of imagining how well you would look in modelling situations from simple snapshots or Polaroids. The most important thing is to take about two to four shots maximum. The first shot should be of your head and shoulders. Face the camera straight on so that people can see you properly. The second should be mid length to your waistline. The third should be full length. Make sure it shows all your body including your feet. This will give a clear indication of your body type and height. The fourth shot should be of your profile. By this I mean stand with your face away from the camera, so the person taking the photo gets a view of the side of your head.

Armed with your snapshots you will now be ready to experience what it is like at a real life casting. This all starts with going to see model agencies. Most agents have what's called an 'open call' or 'walk-in time'. These times can vary, and you will have to look online to find out exactly what the times are. In the UK they are usually between 10am and 12pm and some agents also arrange them for the afternoons from around 2pm–4pm (you can find a full list of top model agencies in the Useful Contacts section of this book). The British Fashion Model Agents Association is a trade association of the UK Model Industry. BFMAA agencies are members of an organisation that denotes their credibility, professionalism and access to top-level clients. This means they will be looking for the best talent. If you use the list and go to see all the agents and are unsuccessful, do not despair. There are many other agents who operate independently and still have access to top fashion clients.

Agencies that are not listed may have a strong presence or they may not, so you might have to do a little more searching to check that they can actually offer you access to the type of jobs you want and can support your career. If you fail to secure an agent the first time, don't give up. Agencies often change like the seasons and what they may not need one season they may well need another. Also, models leave agents and, whilst agencies may already have someone with your look the first time you see them, this could change. So if you're serious, it's well worth waiting a while, perhaps six months, and trying again.

Modelling, like any other industry, is a job. So learn not to take rejection personally. Agents will choose whom they think is most suitable for them. But if nothing else will satisfy your ambition, you can also try agencies in different countries. They may have different requirements or may be slightly more flexible about what they're looking for.

Getting Paid

Most agencies operate a system where you'll be paid on a quarterly system (every three months) but this will depend on the particular agency you're with. Don't be afraid to ask about or chase up payment. Remember: an agent should work as much for you as you should for them.

No reputable fashion agency will ask you for money to join them. Agents make their money from taking commission on jobs that they book you for. Commission can be 15 per cent to 25 per cent of the total sum that you are paid. This is in your favour, as the agent only makes money when they make *you* money. When you become established, you will have more than one agent in different parts of the world. Your first agent will become your 'mother agent' and they will split your commission with the other agent or agencies who get you the job. In other industries, such as acting or if you are a creative talent, you may be charged a nominal fee for your registration or website updates and these can vary.

CHAPTER FOUR

On Camera

ANY PROFESSIONAL photographer worth his salt will know how to direct you, but if you turn up and show that you know what you're doing and are confident, it demonstrates that you're performing your job correctly and are happy to try new things. Before you come to a shoot, be sure to study magazines and advertisements. Look at the poses of the models and don't be scared to imitate them. Practising poses will save time for the client on a shoot, and this can lead to you getting further bookings as they'll realise that if they book you for a job you'll turn up and do it in half the time. If the same client doesn't book you again, it could be because you were too stiff and inhibited. Above all, be yourself and stay true to who you are. Remember: you're like an actor but you're not making a movie. So since you can't use your voice, you must learn to communicate through your facial expressions and – most importantly – with your eyes.

Try thinking about things you love and this will show in the picture, the same way that if you don't think of anything at all, your images are going to come over as flat and lifeless. Before you arrive at the shoot, listen to your favourite music to make you feel relaxed and put you in a good mind-set. Don't forget that you're living the dream. You've secured yourself a photo shoot and it's your chance to shine.

Once you're in the studio, be aware of where the light is. It's really important to make sure that it always hits your face. No matter how you move, your face must always look for the light. And make sure you keep on moving unless the photographer specifically instructs you to do otherwise. Understand that you're trying to give the client as much as possible to work with. If you only strike one pose and retain it throughout, it will limit the entire shoot.

At all times, try to elongate your limbs. If you position your body slightly to the side, so you're standing about three quarters of the way around to the camera and push from the hips, this instantly makes you look slimmer and taller. If you place one foot a little in front of the other and put most of your weight on the back foot, it will give you a longer line on your front leg, as well as giving you better posture. Use your arms. You can cross them, move them towards and around your face and neck or have them simply hanging down. Whatever you do, make sure your hands are relaxed and hold them elegantly. If you put your hands on your hips, the elbow should be slightly back which will make your arms seem longer. Learning different poses will always be helpful, but every shoot is different, and each client may want something you haven't done before. So be prepared to step outside of your comfort zone. Sometimes, when you are in front of the camera, you may find yourself striking a pose that feels awkward to you. Don't let this worry you; go with what the photographer and the client are giving you positive feedback on. After all, you can't see what the image looks like, but they can.

Fashion photographer Ioannis Koussertari defines a top model as:

> Someone who doesn't take themselves seriously. Who brings the energy and plays into the performance. It's the moments when they stop overthinking posing that they become interesting.

CHAPTER FIVE

Where to Start as a Creative

IF YOU DECIDE modelling is not for you, there are so many other areas you can get involved in or create a career from. These include:

Fashion Buyer

A person who attends fashion shows, trade or wholesale showrooms to see the latest work of designers and study trends. They will often work with the designer and the sales team. Their role is extremely important to the business as they will often execute or greatly influence what kinds of stock will be bought for their store or company.

Fashion PR

Public relations in the fashion industry deals with a variety of tasks from talking to the press to coordinating promotions. It usually involves working long or antisocial hours since you must always be ahead of the schedule. The job includes choosing spokes-models, ambassadors and patrons whose work will add value and also be synonymous with the identity of the brand. Many companies respect their PR's decisions and trust them implicitly to promote their brand or their talent. You'll be expected to have a good relationship with the media and be responsible for getting your products placed at the correct events and worn by the right people.

Fashion Writer

This might involve blogging, writing a column for a newspaper or magazine or for your own personal site. The most important thing is your content, as this is what will attract readers, clients and potential clients who may want to commission you to advertise their products or brand. You will be largely reporting on trends as well as the latest fashion design work. So it's important to have good knowledge of the industry and the designers, as well as your target market and what they like to read about. It is becoming increasingly frequent nowadays to witness brands inviting independent writers to their shows and events to promote their new products. Whether you work as part of an established publication or start your own blog, website or social networking page, the most important thing is to get people to read it as often as possible. You'll be continually asked questions such as: 'How many unique visitors do you have per day?' And you will be responsible for creating newsworthy stories around the products, the designer or the company itself.

Styling

Whilst you must be familiar with the trends of the season, the more knowledge of fashion you have the more you can break the rules. Stylists are used on photo shoots, shows, editorials and advertisements, and in many cases the best styling blurs the lines between art and fashion. A stylist will also be in charge of collecting the appropriate accessories, clothing and props. Many celebrities and busy people also employ personal stylists or personal shoppers to select their wardrobe on a daily basis. In any case, understanding body types and the kind of clothing that will best suit the customer is an essential skill.

Presentation Styling ▶

Catwalk Styling ▶

Editorial Styling ▶

Advertising Commercial Styling ▶

Make-up Artist

Make-up artists are an essential part of any shoot or show. You will generally have to take some sort of qualification or attend private lessons to learn about skin types, correct application, contouring and how to manipulate colours to create a specific effect. It's something that you will need to put quite a bit of focus and effort into, but it'll be well worth it and will help you to become brilliant at your job.

Creative Beauty Make-up ▶

Editorial Make-up ▶

Photographer

There are many types of photographers in the fashion industry. They may specialise in one particular field such as commercial, advertising or fashion; or they may work as a press photographer or paparazzi. A photographer who shoots images for a publication will generally be given a budget, a concept and several hours or days to finish the image. Press photographers or paparazzi do the opposite. They take pictures of specified attendees or talent on the day of the show or event. They then circulate the images instantly, usually through an agency such as Getty, Shutterstock and Alamy who will sell them on to the media. Both areas of photography can be lucrative, depending on the individual, and both are extremely competitive and rest largely on the skill of the snapper as well as the quality of the equipment.

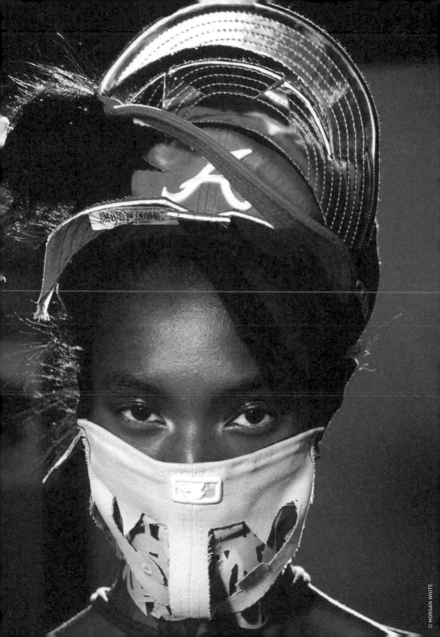

Designer

Most people who want to be a designer will go to a fashion or textile school where they'll learn the techniques of sewing, garment making and sketching (in some rare cases, it's possible to be self-taught.) Generally speaking, a sample will be made of each piece in a collection. The clothing shown in fashion shows is usually what is referred to as couture, which just means you are seeing the piece in its original form and will be handmade. When this has been shown to buyers it may be altered so as to be more suitable for what is called 'ready-to-wear' which basically means the outfits you see and buy on the high street.

Show Producer

To create a great fashion show it's important to have a great show producer. They're the people who are responsible for the mood, lighting, feel and entire energy of the occasion. Big couture houses such as Chanel or Alexander McQueen pride themselves on putting on the most memorable and original shows to generate a talking point around the event and to enthuse their new and existing customers.

Creative Director

This role involves working with designers and marketing companies. A creative director will oversee the vision of the entire shoot to create the appropriate image for the brand. They will also drive the whole team to ensure that the outcome meets the objectives of both the client and the advertising companies.

Sales and Marketing

All designers and fashion houses need people to take care of the sales of their garments to retailers and wholesalers. It's an area where you'll need significant experience in terms of how the industry works, and its etiquette. Some companies may require you to have qualifications such as a degree in Marketing or Business Studies. You will also need an excellent set of contacts and connections across the industry. These will invariably be stockists who will either buy or take your outfits on a sale or return basis.

One of the easiest ways to start your career in the fashion business can be through completing a course at college or university. You might also consider applying for an internship, to be an assistant or an apprentice. An intern is someone who works for a company, on a paid or unpaid basis, in exchange for being taught the specific job that they want to do when they leave that company. This will usually require you to start at the bottom with simple tasks and work your way up within the organisation depending on how long the placement is for. Volunteering to work as an assistant at an upcoming or established creative talent is a great way to get your foot in the door and prove your commitment, reliability and professionalism. It can also mean the opportunity to work with someone who is at the very top of their career. The job may not be financially rewarding, but it's a chance to pick up an ocean of experience.

An apprenticeship is where you learn or gain recognised qualifications and skills while you're being paid to do the job. Often, you will be taught directly by a specific individual or professional. And it may also include periodic assessment or tests to ensure you're learning as you go. It's a brilliant and practical way to really grow into your chosen field and it'll mean you're earning the national minimum wage.

The Importance of Setting Goals

Identify Your Goal

It may seem obvious, but one of the most crucial considerations in the success or failure of your objective is deciding exactly what it is you want to achieve and then working backwards to identify specifically how to move forward. For example, you may want to be a model, but first you must decide precisely what kind of model – advertising, editorial, or catwalk? You'll then be able to work out what you need to do to achieve your ambition.

Research Your Path

Since you've chosen to read this book, you clearly understand that, to gain the tools, skills and experience you'll need to do the job you want, you'll need to do a certain amount of research. Through doing this, you'll be better equipped to make yourself as appealing as possible to the agents or companies that you'd like to work with.

Create Your Strategy

Once you have identified your goal and done your research, you'll then be able to create a strategy around how you wish to achieve your desired goal. This might mean making sure you attend the appropriate events, workshops and talks by industry professionals. And if being a fashion creative is your aim, you should consider taking a course at a college or university or working as an intern at a fashion house or magazine.

Plan Your Steps

It's very important to plan your steps and your preferred outcome. This will allow you to worry less, as you will have a comprehensive and documented account of what you are doing and where you are going. Think about creating a folder where you can collect all the information that you need to achieve your goal. And keep a diary to plan the specific dates by which you'd like to achieve each part of your strategy. This will help you to remain focused and stay on track.

Choose What is Right for You

Many people tend not to think about who they are as a person and how that might work from an ethical perspective regarding what work they will and won't do. If you intend to be a model, it is vital to understand exactly what the industry will demand from you and if you will be comfortable in those situations. That may have a bearing on your entire strategy and the kind of model you want to be.

Affirm Your Success

When you are finally successful in achieving your goals, take some time to affirm or enjoy your successes. That doesn't just mean when you finally land yourself a major campaign. Even just getting the opportunity to go and see designers or clients means you are beginning to live your dream.

Be Grateful and Thankful

Once you're on your way, stop and think every now and then to reflect on how many people are trying to achieve the same goal as you but who may not have achieved quite as much. Be thankful and grateful for every opportunity that comes your way and to anyone who helps you progress. Spend time during the day or at night to acknowledge your development and to appreciate your discipline and dedication.

Create a Goal Book

This is simply a means of defining a goal or set of goals and putting them into visible form. Use a notebook or ring binder folder and make it as detailed and colourful as you want it to be. Put together a collage of pictures from old magazines; add dates, photographs and details of how you have already achieved some of those goals.

Ensure that you spend a minimum of 15 minutes a day visualising your goals as complete, and living the kind of life you want to have. This might mean five minutes over a three-hour period, or first thing in the morning, in the afternoon and at night. If you keep your goal book handy, it will help you to have specific dates to work to. This is all about time management and organisation.

Decide when you can work and when you can't so that you're clear about when and how you'll be able to realise your ambitions. And as you start creating your goal book, give some thought to answering the following questions:

Exercise One

- What do I really want to achieve?

- What makes me happy?

- If I could work anywhere in the world where would it be?

- Who inspires me?

- What kind of modelling do I want to do?

- Do I want to work as a fashion creative?

- Am I more interested in the business of fashion?

- Do I need more experience or training?

CHAPTER SIX
Building Your Portfolio

ONCE YOU'VE SECURED yourself an agent, they will set you up with a top photographer and styling team. However, if you don't have an agent, you can still create a portfolio by way of 'test shoots'. But be careful; doing too many shoots like this can lead you to lose your exclusivity. Think of yourself as having value. And bear in mind that for every test shoot you do you're taking something away from your brand. If, in the future, clients want to book you, the last thing they want to know or see is that you've done lots of unpaid and unpublished work, which may not even show you at your very best.

As with any job, you need to know what is expected of you and how to present yourself. So do not rush into anything. Read fashion magazines and look at agency websites so you can see exactly what it is you're aspiring to. This will also help you to work out the correct postures and poses that the client is looking for. The very best images convey an emotion. This can range from strong and authoritarian to elation, happiness or even vulnerability. Supermodels completely command their space and practise tirelessly and regularly.

Should you choose to contact a photographer and arrange a test shoot (or TFP as they're called in the industry) try to get them to take both outdoor and indoor images and make sure you choose pictures that show you at your best. No one has time to work out how you might look if you'd had a little more sleep. You will be judged purely on those pictures. Always stay on good terms with photographers, makeup artists, hairdressers and stylists. They may be the ones booking you for paid work in the future.

Also, if you're doing a test shoot, take cuttings from established magazines and send these images to the photographer and the rest of the team so that they can see what you need. Be extremely selective about who you work with. Remember: you don't need hundreds of photographs. You only need a few that show your best features. If you're signed to an agency, let them select the photographers that you'll be working with. This will ensure you get the quality of images required to sell your 'look' in the proper way. Ask your booker (the person at your agency who looks after you) for advice if you are in doubt about anything, such as posing etc. Again, if you don't have an agent, the key is to be selective. There's no point paying huge amounts of money for images that may not be as good as you need them to be.

The Correct Attitude

It's incredibly important to have the correct attitude when you're on a job. As human beings, we are naturally protective of our image and how people perceive us. And in this industry, clients will want and will be paying to control that image to fulfil their vision for their brand. For example, you may arrive at a shoot and they may put you in bright orange clothing, rainbow shoes, and green lipstick. You might well feel uncomfortable wearing all it, which will of course affect your attitude. If this happens it can very bad for your reputation, as people won't understand. They'll just think you're moody or have a bad attitude. If you're not happy about something, remember to remain professional and state exactly what your issue is. If you really feel it's against your personal core beliefs, then try to make the team aware as soon as possible or get in touch with your agency. But if you decide to do the shoot, then you must also bear in mind that very often you're not seeing the full picture. You're only seeing you and that's not from behind the camera where the photographer can see all the elements – set, styling, props and background – in place at the same time to make the scene come to life. Don't forget that whether you think you're right or not, there are others around you who have vast experience in doing their job. When you complain unnecessarily or without a valid reason you are undermining *their* job. It's not acceptable to demand a change of outfit, make-up or a hairstyle after you've had it done for your job. This will just make people unwilling to work with you again.

Although you may feel modelling is not the same as a desk job, it's even more important to show that you are professional, reliable and polite, and keep good time. If, for some reason, you have an issue on the job or at a casting, say nothing. Instead, tell your agency who can take it up on your behalf. You may be justified, but it's very easy to get a bad reputation in this business. Please refer to the *Legislations and Unions* section later in this chapter. Above all, be kind and try to have a great relationship with everyone you work with. If you do, people will remember you in a good way and book you again in the future.

Fashion Director Kim Howells of Rankin's *Hunger* magazine advises:

> Modelling for me is all about the right vibe, confidence and understanding and enjoying who you are. Knowing yourself on camera,

understanding how the clothes look and what can be achieved always elevates a shoot.

Castings

One of the biggest mistakes most models make is over-dressing, wearing unnecessary make-up or being ostentatious. This can also stop you from being scouted in your everyday life since no one would dare walk up to someone in the street and ask them to remove their makeup and high heels. It's important for you to understand that the client wants to see the real you in your natural form. This can be daunting but it is part of being confident in yourself and in your own beauty. Your natural beauty will exude confidence to any new client you meet and encourages them to be able to imagine you with different looks and in different settings. Through time, you will develop your own style. But if you're not sure what to wear, you should always have the following in your kitbag: a pair of flat shoes or trainers, a pair of black heels, a plain white vest top and a pair of skinny jeans. It may seem simple, but to be honest, it's the best outfit for attending casting sessions or going to see an agency. And the best part is, it's easy to wear, not expensive and will show your best features. You can also opt for a simple dress if you like, but make sure it's not too fussy and complements the season. So if it's summer, go for lighter colours and if it's winter go for darker colours. No matter what you wear though, make sure it's comfortable and easy to get in and out of. This is because at castings, clients may want you to try something on there and then. Models are usually happy to do this as they're so used to getting changed backstage. If you're uncomfortable however, politely state this to the client. If you do, make sure you feel confident to ask if there is a private space where you can change. If they refuse, then it's completely up to you whether or not you go ahead. Good clients will always provide a safe environment for you to change. Never, ever, be coerced into anything that you do not want to do. It's your life and it's important that you live it the way you want to.

Make sure you do everything you possibly can to be on time. This might be difficult sometimes, but the more castings you attend the more opportunities you'll have to get a job. As a model, you can often be sent to many different parts of the world where more than likely you won't have a driver or chaperone. When you arrive in any new city, buy a local and city map. Be sure to download any relevant apps if you have a smart phone or tablet; this will help you navigate the city. If you receive your castings in advance, take the time to use sites such as Google Maps or City Mapper to plan your journey before you leave home. Check the weather forecasts so that you know if you can take public transport. If the location is close enough, you may want to take a taxi to avoid looking harassed or tired. Finally, research the designer or the brand; this will help you to indulge in some light conversation and prove to the client that you enjoy their work.

Diversity in the Fashion Industry

In 2015 Jourdan Dunn became the first black model in over 12 years to be featured on the cover of British *Vogue*. This brought up many concerns about how the fashion industry has been operating. It seems obvious, though, that the industry reflects wider views held within society, which unfortunately are shaped by the world's colonial past.

It was reported by the *Diversity Journal* in October 2012 that, during New York Fashion Week 2012, of the 4,708 looks shown, just 20.6 per cent were modelled by women of colour. Of these, 8.1 per cent were black and 10.1 per cent were Asian. What is most disturbing though is that only 1.9 per cent were from Latino backgrounds. According to the 2010 Census, Latinos make-up 16.35 per cent of the US population and are the largest single minority group in America.[2]

Regardless of race or class, you should never, ever be put off your dream in any industry. However, keep in mind that if you are a person of colour, or have a non-traditional look, you may experience more rejection depending on which part of the world you are based. You must understand this so that you don't doubt your own ability, talent or beauty.

Industry expert Caryn Franklin MBE (Psych) MBPs, Fashion and Identity Commentator and Professor of Diversity at Kingston University defines a model as follows:

> A good model is someone who can empower others to feel excited about being human. In an ideal world and because we need to see a diverse spectrum of appearance and self-hood, this model will be part of a modelling culture that celebrates all body types, age variations, skin tones and physical difference.

It is imperative that models, designers, stylists, make-up artists, and everyone else who is employed in the fashion industry join together to change this imbalance. In fact, some leading designers – Vivienne Westwood for example – have been constantly striving to create a fairer reflection of what is termed 'beautiful' through the unconventionality of their collections and the diversity of their models.

At the same time, we're seeing more and more companies following the example of The Body Shop, who's founder Dame Anita Roddick believed that big business should be a force for good and that it should 'enrich not exploit'. She was an incredibly powerful environmental campaigner and businesswoman who sought to create a brand that was focused on ethical consumption. To this day, The Body Shop is completely committed to a series of pledges and targets that aim to help the planet. These include ensuring that their stores run on 100 per cent renewable or carbon balanced energy; helping 40,000 economically challenged people around the world; developing new sustainable packaging and building bio bridges that protect 750 million square metres of habitat so that, by 2020, communities can live more sustainably. Other individuals promoting sustainability are philanthropist Olivia Firth, who founded Eco Age to help support businesses to become more sustainable, and journalist and writer Lucy Seigle. While attending National Earth Day I was introduced to Lucy and, as a leading voice on the impact on the environment of our current consumption behaviour, she adds the following on to this topic:

It was over a decade ago when I began researching the environmental footprint of what was in my wardrobe, I think people thought I was crazy. 'Why does it matter?' they would ask, while at the same time fanatically researching the provenance of every ingredient they ate. Carrots needed to be organic, but t-shirts… not so much. In the early 1990s a chain store brand that was once a stalwart on the UK high street introduced an organic cotton range of clothing. Consumers were mystified by the 'organic cotton' labelling. Some asked shop assistants if it was edible.

It is thanks to pioneers like the fashion designer, Katharine Hamnett, that we are not all standing around in shops chewing trouser legs in total confusion. Hamnett was one of the first designers to make the point that fashion is a full spectrum industry that contains many steps and many inputs of natural resources, especially water. The fashion supply chain is not just designers and models and influencers (all the exciting instagrammable stuff) but also millions of farmers and producers who coax the fibre from plants from the ground. Fashion uses millions of litres of water, not just in the growing of fibre (cotton is known to be one the world's thirstiest plants) but in the dyeing and finishing processes. We also use fabric from tree bark, so fashion involves foresters and wool from animals raised on grasslands, including the vulnerable Alashan Planes of Mongolia which are now under pressure from huge cashmere goat herds.

In fact, outside of farming, it's hard to think of an industry that owes a greater debt to planet Earth than fashion. It exerts a huge pressure on the Earth. Every year we now produce over 100 billion new garments, almost all from virgin (new) resources. To add insult to injury, the average lifespan of a garment is in freefall, and we throw away often to landfill or for incineration (modern clothes are complicated to recycle). 'Waste' piles on yet more pressure on to the biosphere: clothes in landfill produce greenhouse gases which accelerates climate change and burning clothing produces dioxins which poison life sustaining systems.

Every year the Earth-defending charity holds World Overshoot Day. This is held on the day that statistically we exceed the Earth's capacity to regenerate life-sustaining resources. It's not exactly cause for celebration; in 2017 it fell on 2 August and every year it creeps forward by a few days. The goal is to push it back. But fashion with its huge ecological footprint pushes us further in to the red!

The rise of sustainable fashion, driven originally by Katharine Hamnett (as I mentioned), shows that the design and fashion community are addressing this head on. Hamnett made the point that cotton was ecologically indefensible as a fibre because it is not only seriously thirsty but also uses a large amount of the world's pesticides. Instead of perpetuating this enviro-craziness, and pushing the planet into the red, she called on designers and brands to use organic cotton – free of the pesticide burden. As the movement grew and more sustainable fashion brands began to appear that let the planet set the limits, more and more consumers have come to understand why fashion's environmental footprint is important.

Over ten years on from my initial research, and a number of books and documentaries down, I no longer have to begin every conversation explaining the connection between fashion and the planet. In fact the idea of a sustainable, planet friendly wardrobe is accelerating beyond my wildest dreams. Organic cotton now seems a first-rung remedy.

We are entering a fibre revolution, where we will finally break the stranglehold of cotton (produced cheaply) and oil-based synthetics. In recent times we have seen leathers made of apple and organic skins and fish skins come to market, and even garments that are made from silks 'brewed' in laboratories. We have seen futuristic denim that uses tiny amounts of water and the implementation of a protocol to cover the use and processing of 'forest fibres' to make sure that old growth forests that are important wildlife habitats are not sacrificed for fashion.

Lucy Siegle

Much more needs to be done by the fashion industry as a whole to ensure that our lifestyle and consumption patterns function in a way that is not detrimental to the planet.

Katharine Hamnett 2018 ▶

Legislation & Unions

In 2017, two of the world's largest luxury fashion groups, LVMH and Kering, released a report to the world called 'The Charter on Working Relations with Fashion Models'.[3] This was an acknowledgement of the frequently poor working conditions that are part of the fashion industry. At the same time, it was an opportunity to address and improve the situation. Equity, the UK's leading organisation for the protection of performing artists and models, has done a lot of work in this area particularly in relation to tackling problems with agents, and restrictions on the use of models under 16. In the Equity Ten Point Code the union articulates several more concerns in detail, such as making sure models are paid on time and the kinds of working conditions that are acceptable or suitable to work in. As models and creative people it is crucial that such issues are robustly debated, and that practical means are set up to ensure that there is appropriate legislation to protect individuals.

Staying Safe While at Work

There's no reason on earth why you should be expected to work in conditions that make you feel scared, violated or embarrassed, regardless of your gender. If you want to be a model, try to join a reputable agency and avoid any work that is not booked directly by them. If you're on set and have a serious problem and feel that you can't confront the client or worse, tell your booker at the agency and then join a union so that you can make anonymous or direct complaints. It's very important that any incidents are reported to protect models in the industry and the same rules should also apply for any other professional environment.

Exercise Two

- Where do I fit within the industry?

- What kind of a model or creative do I want to be?

- What are my strengths?

- What are my weaknesses?

- How can I achieve balance to be successful in my chosen career path?

CHAPTER SEVEN
Dealing With Rejection

THERE IS NO point in blaming yourself for not getting a particular job, simply because there are so many different reasons why you may or may not have been picked. These could include which agency you are with, your physical build, your hair type, your ethnicity, your personality or if the designer has a very specific 'look' that they are seeking. They may want someone with a more typical appearance or someone who is quirkier. The only thing you can do is to be sure that you are fully prepared before you attend. Part of being prepared is ensuring the way you think is positive and that you feel you deserve the opportunity. This doesn't mean you should take your ego into the room with you. It simply means making sure that your mental state is such that you're in good spirits.

As a model, you will have to go to every single casting with this positive attitude and make sure you leave any issues behind you. Even if you're not picked, don't feel down or sad about it. Yes, I know this is hard – especially if you really want the job. But if you carry the disappointment to the next casting you won't get that job either.

If you do make a mistake, learn from it and don't repeat the same action. And if you happen to do it again, try not to punish yourself. Just promise yourself you'll do better next time.

Talent is not always enough to get booked. Character, patience and maturity are helpful too. Everyone has doubts, but it is essential to deal with overriding negative thoughts and replace them with positive ones. Allow yourself to focus on happy experiences before, during and after castings. Understand that if you are there, you are in fact living your dream. Don't allow things that have not happened to ruin the reality of the situation. Be true to yourself and never change who you are, especially if it means doing something that you do not feel comfortable with. You may come into the industry and decide it is not for you. Don't be disappointed. Be happy that you have learned and experienced what you wished for.

People say the means justify the end. But no amount of success, money or title will erase the memory of doing something that goes against your core beliefs. By core beliefs, what I mean are the things that you believe in, that you would feel bad about if you transgressed.

Look at modelling for what it is. In many cases, most models will not become working models, let alone super-models. But if you have the right attitude, the right look and positive motivation as well as determination, you will make it. Decide what success means to you. It might just be landing an international or national campaign, or being on your favourite magazine front cover. Don't let other people define it for you, as most of the time their expectations will be unreasonable or so far beyond what you really need to be happy and live well.

Never judge or compare yourself with someone else. Stay focused on yourself and make sure you are not distracted or allowing negative emotions to stop you from getting to where you want to be. If you don't get the job, keep trying, stay positive and realise that just because you were not picked the first, second or third time you may be chosen the fourth time. The client you have gone to see may not think you are appropriate for one job, but they may have you in mind for something else. Like anything in life, there will be moments where you will feel you are not good enough. But when you truly understand the beauty of being human, no matter what anyone says or does, you will appreciate that all humans are incredible creatures and no job can ever define that.

Supermodel Richard Biedul, who is signed to some of the top agencies in the world, including Marilyn and Elite, says:

> Historically there were parameters such as height, weight, and age, but now these restrictions have slowly and thankfully been eroded away over the last 10 years. The beauty of the industry is the diversity now exists within. Mental confidence and respect for others, and most importantly yourself, is a great starting point. But these are probably not enough. An interest in fashion helps but is not essential. A drive to succeed and a determination to show your personality over and above just your look in a sea of beautiful people will stand you in great stead in this industry.

The fashion industry is based around two seasons: the first being Autumn Winter (referred to as A/W) and the second being Spring Summer (referred to as S/S). And just like the weather, these seasons change continuously. What might be in one season may be out the next. Trends within the wider world and the environment can also influence what a client is looking for at any one moment in time, so again you may not be chosen one year but you could be the next. A perfect example of this was the surge in 2015 for real models with non-typical looks such as the albino model Shaun Ross, Winnie Harlow who confidently teaches the world about the rare skin condition Vitiligo; and hijab model Halima Aden. In the past, it would have been virtually impossible for such models to be the face of a major international fashion campaign.

You might also be surprised to know that all models during events such as London Fashion Week can often find themselves commuting from four to ten castings a day and only be booked for a few of those jobs. You can only do your best. If you look as good as you can, have dressed appropriately, have the right attitude and you are still not picked, understand that the client has a different vision for the brand.

Overcoming Obstacles

Throughout your career and personal life, there will be obstacles and hurdles you will have to overcome. If it's possible to change the situation, it can be referred to as a hurdle since there's an opportunity to get around or over it. These may include things such as where you live, your education and training, the level of enthusiasm that you show, being professional and respectful, having a sense of grace, or the kind of people you spend time with. An obstacle on the other hand, is something that you cannot change. This could be a family member who requires your care, dependents or children, your height, skin colour, core beliefs or body type. It is essential to identify which obstacles in your life can be changed and which you will have to learn to work with and not against. Again, a really great way to help you to achieve your ambitions is by using your goal book.

Exercise Three

- Do I plan to build a portfolio before I go to see agents or clients?

- What steps can I take to make sure I have the correct attitude?

- How can I ensure I stay positive before and after interviews or castings?

CHAPTER EIGHT

Social Media and Fashion

IT'S NOW COMMON practice for agents to expect you to post online in a certain way and even credit the people you have worked with, however personal it may be. In some cases, your agency may even want to run your social media platforms for you, which may not be optional. So be aware that if you do have a profile you will be judged on what you post. Many believe that this is unethical but in our online world, it's often the first port of call for many bookers and clients. With that in mind, here are some tips:

- You should only post pictures that reflect your best side.

- Learn how to work with the camera to get your best angles and poses.

- If you have a great photo shoot, post one image on your site every other day. If you post too many you will not achieve as much engagement since most viewers will only really focus or comment on one image at a time.

- Try to post a variety of images that are not just of you looking good. You don't want people to think of you as being vain.

- Post images of your hobbies and talents. This will show people that there's more to you than just being a model.

- If you want to attract new followers try posting at different times of the day so that you feed into other countries' time zones.

- Be careful what you post. Your profile on your model agency website might be brilliant, but if you then post images that contradict that or which might upset potential brands or sponsors, they won't be able to use you.

As a stylist, photographer or designer the same applies. You must present the image of your brand as if it's a fully functioning website. So show the best work you have and display it to the max. Many people have made a lucrative career from blogging and posting videos discussing other people's work. This demonstrates the potential to grow your business and your brand through social media. Do not take it for granted, but recognise it as a brilliant opportunity for you to bring your work to the world. What's more, you can build your own following in a way that is now no longer dominated by PR agents and big brands on the high street.

CHAPTER NINE
Health and Nutrition

EVEN IF YOU already have the correct body type for the kind of modelling that you're best suited to, it's very important to look after your heath with a balanced and nutritious diet. Working as a model is highly competitive and extremely exhausting work so you must eat the right things to stay healthy. It can also make the difference between getting a job and not. For example, if a client is casting and two models attend who have a similar look, the next thing they will look at is the health of your skin, nails, hair and teeth. You could have the best look in the world, but if you don't look after these important areas of the body you won't get the job.

There has been considerable controversy over the years about super-skinny models and those who have fainted or collapsed on jobs. If you're not looking after your general health and nutrition and you are working intensely, it could lead to you becoming ill. This will be devastating for your career and may even result in you being dropped. So love yourself, look after yourself and exercise regularly. If the gym or running are not your thing, or you have a slight frame that you want to preserve, try exercises such as Pilates which will encourage the development of what in science are called 'long muscles'. These muscles develop with exercise that stretches and holds the muscle for a long period and are brilliant for your physical strength, giving you definition that is not too muscular. Exercising will also help you to stay motivated and focused.

It's a popular myth that not eating keeps you skinny. This is something that is practiced not only by some models but also by many people in wider society. Scientifically, not eating has the opposite effect. What happens is when you don't eat your body starts to panic and, because your body has gone into this state, anything you eat at all will instantly be converted to fat and stored by your body. This is because your body is not sure when the next meal will arrive. In this sense, it is much better and easier to have a balanced diet, but you must eat at regular specific times. This will train your body to get into a habit where it knows when you will have a meal. What happens then is your body will work harder to burn up the fat since it knows that in a few hours' time you will be eating again.

When it comes to your health and general wellbeing, do not underestimate the incredible benefits of walking. Start your day as early as possible. Six am is a brilliant time to rise when everything is lovely and quiet and everyone else is usually still asleep. It's a time of day that instantly instils a feeling of clarity and it's an opportunity for you to think about your ambitions, your life and the job at hand. Rising early and taking a long walk is not only great for your health and for your body, but especially for your mental wellbeing. To make it in the fashion industry or indeed in any part of the entertainment world you must be completely focused and balanced in your mind and body. Have something small to eat such as a piece of fruit and perhaps some carbohydrates such as porridge, bran, oats or brown bread – depending on your dietary requirements. This will give you strength to complete your walk without feeling disoriented or down. And don't forget to take a bottle of water with you. Keeping hydrated is crucial.

There are also many important scientific and biological reasons why walking is good for you:[4]

- Engages your abdominal muscles

- Improves balance

- Improves blood pressure

- Strengthens legs
- Limits colon cancer by 31 per cent in women
- Halves the risk of Alzheimer's disease
- Reduces the risk of glaucoma
- Boosts endorphins

Walking burns more fat than jogging, which can have a dangerous impact on your joints and especially your knees. And the benefits I've just mentioned above are very real and are exactly what your body needs for you to be the best that you can be.

When you work in the fashion industry you'll be constantly on your feet, going from one casting session to another, doing fashion shows, and often posing in awkward surroundings and locations. The relentless schedule, which can include travelling frequently by plane, will all take its toll on your body. So if you have some spare time, try to find out if there are any local dance classes or activities that can help you wind down. This is beneficial not only from an aerobic and anaerobic perspective, but it's also a fun way for you to get the exercise and tone that you need. Learning how to dance well will also help you to lose your inhibitions and anxieties.

Bodyworks

Commonwealth Games gymnastics gold medallist Steve Frew is an esteemed athlete and personal trainer. He's worked with some of the top athletes in the world as well as clients from all walks of life. He has developed a training programme specifically for models. Gymnastics is a bodyweight exercise, which involves movements that form the foundation of all sports and develop strength, balance, flexibility, coordination, speed, agility and stamina. These key skills, combined with high intensity cardiovascular exercise and a healthy well-balanced diet, will help you achieve an incredible figure, focusing on the following areas:

- Long Lean Muscle Toning

- Core and Abdominal Training

- Resistance Training Exercises

- High Intensity Cardiovascular Exercise (Interval Training)

- Maintaining Peak Fitness at Work

As a fashion model, your career naturally depends on the way you look. So it stands to reason that exercise is important to improve posture and muscle tone, as well as control body fat. Exercise also increases your mental health and wellbeing through releasing endorphins – powerful feel-good chemicals in your brain, which energise your spirit and uplift your mood.

Long Lean Muscle Toning

Correct posture exudes confidence and encourages stability while walking the runway, giving the model a level of grace and flow of movement. Once learned, this can then be deconstructed and adapted to specific clients or the energy of the show. One of the main ways to improve your posture is through muscle toning. Stretching and increasing the length of the muscle provides a healthy range of motion in the joints and helps to reduce injuries. As a result, you have greater control over your body and your movements.

Always warm up first and make sure you perform each exercise with caution, especially if you're a beginner. Keep a bottle of water with you.

Elbow Plank-Reverse Leg Lift

Start in an elbow plank position. Slowly raise one leg as high as you feel comfortable, whilst trying to keep your back in the original position. Hold the stretch for as long as possible, and then lower to the ground. Repeat on the opposite leg. Try to do 16 repetitions. Then rest for ten to 30 seconds and perform the whole routine twice or in two sets. (16 reps x 2 sets)

Slow Single Leg V-Sit

Start by lying on your back with your hands straight up above your head. Lift your upper body to a sitting position. Raise one leg and hold the stretch. Then slowly lower the leg and upper body to the ground and repeat with the other leg (12 reps x 2/3 sets).

Picture in your mind a big panther-like cat. Visualise the way it appears to almost float across the ground as it walks. It controls each leg movement with grace, and authority, and with incredible stability. But it is poised, knowing exactly where and when to place each powerful step. This is the level of awareness and body-control a model should aspire to.

Ballet, Pilates, yoga, and gymnastics are brilliant for long and lean muscle training. Activities like these empower both models and athletes to fine-tune their bodies, and also work creatively with the mind.

Core and Abdominal Toning

Young gymnasts must first learn to control and master their own bodyweight before they can learn any of the more advanced skills. It's the ultimate display of core strength and they rarely ever use any free-weights in development.

Instead, they achieve this by using their own natural body weight to strengthen and tone the core and abdominals. As a model, a relatively strong core helps you stretch and pose in ways which will lift your career on camera and give you more of an in depth understanding of your body. By improving your core and abdominal strength, you'll have greater balance and so much more control when shooting editorials or walking on runways.

The following exercises can be combined into a sequence; do however feel free to add your own variations. And always work at a level that suits you best.

Front Support Plank

Hold your shoulders above your hands, squeezing your buttocks and feet together. Maintain the position without sagging through your spine, dropping your hips, or rotating your back. Do this for 30 seconds to begin with, then build up to one-minute x 3 sets. If you find this too difficult, try elbow plank holds instead before building up to straight-arm holds.

Side Support Planks

From a front support plank, rotate your body and place one arm alongside as shown in the picture. Hold for 10 seconds, then place your arm on the floor whilst

rotating your body and hold the position using the opposite arm for 10 seconds. Your shoulder should be directly above your hands, and your body should be aligned and straight without sagging at the hips. Squeeze your legs and feet tightly together and keep your head in a neutral position. Do three sets of each sequence.

Back Support

From an L-shaped sitting position, place your hands on the floor. Press your chest upwards as high as possible without sagging, and slide your feet forward as shown in the picture. Your shoulders should be directly above your hands, with your legs straight and your feet held firmly together. You can bend your knees to make the position easier if necessary. Hold for 30 seconds x 3 sets.

Sit Up Variation

Lay flat on your back with your knees bent at 90 degrees, then slowly lift your head and shoulders. Fix and hold this position for two to five seconds. Then

slowly lower back to a flat position on the mat. Do
10–12 reps x 3 sets.

The core unites the upper and lower body, and a strong
core will join the two in harmony. Working your core
is a fantastic way to achieve more defined muscle tone,
and this is particularly helpful for fitness models.

Resistance Training Exercises

If you're serious about becoming a model, it makes sense
to combine strength training with functional fitness

exercises or routines using resistance bands and body weight (or 'force') to give you appropriate resistance. This helps to tone and define your lean muscles so that you look great during shooting.

Here are a few exercises using your body as a 'force':

Dish Hold

Lie on your back with your hands by your side. Now lift your shoulders and feet off the ground at the same time. Try to keep your lower back as flat as possible on the mat. Then lengthen and elongate your arms. Fix and hold the position for 10 seconds and relax. Repeat x 5 sets.

Superhero Dorsal Raises

Lie face down on a mat with your hands above shoulders. Lift and raise your arms off the ground and lift and raise your feet off the ground, squeezing your feet together. Hold position for 10 seconds x 5 reps. Straddle your legs to make the position easier.

These two exercises can be combined. Start with the dish position, and then roll into the superhero position.

High Intensity Interval Training

HIIT or High Intensity Interval Training is great for cardiovascular fat burning fitness. The advantage with HIIT is that you can do it anytime, anywhere – even whilst travelling. It doesn't require an expensive gym or fancy equipment, just a small space and a little time.

HIIT includes exercises such as planking, squats, lunges, burpees, mountain-climbers, star jumps, and shuttle runs. These exercises work by raising your heart rate to between 75–90 per cent of its maximum. Within this range you'll be reducing or 'burning' body fat, whilst simultaneously increasing your muscular endurance, strength and stamina. Perform each exercise for 30 seconds then rest for 30 seconds. Aim to achieve as many repetitions of the exercise as possible, before moving onto the next exercise, and try and complete five circuits. You can do this routine over a five, ten, 15, 20 or even a 30-minute timeslot, whatever your schedule allows.

Mountain Climbers

Start in a front support position, keeping your glutes downwards towards the floor, and ensuring your back is straight and flat. Drive your knees one at a time towards your chest as if you're climbing and repeat this movement as quickly as you feel comfortable with.

Long Lunges

Stand with your legs together. Lift one leg with a bent knee and place the foot forward into a lunging position. Then press with the leading leg to stand up straight again. Change the leading leg and repeat the exercise. Make sure your leading leg knee doesn't extend over your toes, and that your back knee doesn't touch the ground.

Squat Pulses

From a standing start, place your feet shoulder-width apart or at a distance that's comfortable for you. Then lower yourself into a chair position and bend upwards and downwards, keeping your body in a squat pose and placing tension in your quadriceps.

Long Straddle

Lie flat on your back, and then lift your shoulders and feet off the floor into a dish position as shown in the

picture. With your hands forward, open your legs into a straddle posture and then close them back to a dish and repeat, making sure you keep your feet off the ground.

Maintaining Peak Fitness at Work

Focus on Short-Term Goals

Concentrate on an upcoming event or a fashion show. Just having something that you know is coming up that you can work towards will give you an incentive. Your goal then becomes a target to aim towards and the closer you get to your target, the more your motivation will build.

Most athletes focus on short-term goals. It helps them to take some of the pressure off whilst staying committed to their long-term plans.

Create a Reward System

When you reach an agreed target with your training, reward yourself with a prize. This could be anything from enjoying a fun night out with friends to spending a long weekend away, or just treating yourself to something special.

Train with a Friend

If you feel your motivation starting to slack, train with a friend or colleague. It seems really simple, but it's a really good way to maintain your enthusiasm. It also means you can support each other on those days when all you want to do is stay at home in bed.

Fitness That Works For You

We're all individuals and respond to different things in different ways. Likewise, no two body systems are the same. So it's important to identify what works best for you, and how it makes you feel.

Be Organised

Ever heard the expression 'failing to plan is planning to fail'? It's absolutely crucial that you think ahead. The fashion schedule is extremely intense from week to week during Spring Summer and Autumn Winter; so make sure you plan your gym hours beforehand. That way, you'll always show up at castings and shoots looking your best.

Travel Organised

Be sure to include your trainers, a skipping rope, resistance bands and any other portable gear you own when you pack your suitcase. This means you can keep up your fitness routine and workout anywhere whilst travelling.

Make exercise fun and creative

There are so many different ways to exercise. For example, one hour spent at a trampoline centre will give you really high levels of cardiovascular exercise and is super fun, exciting and anything but boring. Or you could go to a dance class, ski, skate, surf, hula-hoop, paddleboard…

whatever. There are so many options out there. But the most important thing is to enjoy what you do. This will help you cope with the downsides to the industry such as rejection and keep you bubbly and working to your optimal level.

CHAPTER TEN

Supermodel Tips

- Never do anything that goes against who you are as a person. Neither money nor fame can ever remove or replace your dignity.

- Don't be afraid to believe in yourself. If you don't believe in yourself, how can you expect anyone else to?

- Love yourself and understand that you are in a highly competitive industry. Like a professional footballer, you'll struggle to earn a professional contract and find an agent. And even then, you'll get transferred and undergo many trials before you eventually get to where you want to be.

- Decide whether you want fame because you love the art form or because you want to work and earn an income. This can influence your path.

- Never care too much what anyone thinks of you other than your agent and the client.

Fellow models can be jealous or exclusive, as they may have worked a lot harder than you to get to where they are. So don't expect to be welcomed in.

- Find an agent who believes in you. There are many girls with top companies who may work a lot less than others from smaller agencies. It's imperative that your booker believes in you and wants to see you succeed; otherwise you'll end up fading into the background. Understand that agencies will usually put their own interests before yours. And, depending on your age, try to think about what you might be able to do in terms of work should your model agency ever drop you.

- Never put anyone else down and never let anyone destroy your dream. Recognise that people will feel threatened by you and they may want to test you. Perseverance, dedication, kindness and humbleness will keep you on the right road and teach you the most.

- With modelling also comes access to high profile events and parties. Beware of intoxicants of any nature as they can ruin your life and your career.

- Always have your book and comp cards ready. Always.

- Less is more. You do not need to wear make-up at all when you are casting or seeing agents. They want to see the real you.

CHAPTER ELEVEN

The A to Z of Happy Healthy Eating

Avocado

Avocado is a particularly good food as it can be consumed at any time of day. It's packed with lots of yummy goodness to help you feel fit and healthy. It's also great for your general wellbeing.

Avocado is full of vitamin K, vitamin B6, Potassium and Omega 3:

- Vitamin K is a very important nutrient because it aids the process of blood clotting which in turn helps to heal wounds when we're injured and encourages healthy bone development.

- Vitamin B6 helps your brain send vital signals for communication throughout the body as well as helping to convert food into energy – and that needs to be done every day.

- Potassium is a highly significant mineral that improves brain function and can help to control blood pressure and sugar levels. That means healthier cell tissue and organ function.

- Omega 3 is a healthy fat, which can reduce inflammation in the body. So all in all, the humble avocado is an easy and great way to not only look after your insides but also maintain lovely glowing skin.

Tip: Cream avocado for an instant facemask.

Broccoli

- This vastly underestimated vegetable is extremely high in fibre, so reducing the risk of heart disease, strokes and even hypertension. It can also help to lower cholesterol.

- Broccoli contains vitamin C as well as anti-oxidants that can help fight skin damage caused by the sun and pollution. It can also reduce the appearance of ageing skin to leave you looking younger and more beautiful.

Coconut
This has got to be one of the most versatile fruits on the planet. You can buy coconut soap and coconut cream, plus many other coconut-based products that are now essential to maintaining our lifestyles.

- Coconut oil is a great healthy oil. It consists of long-chain fatty acids, which are metabolised differently from those found in red meat or cheese.

- It contains ketones too, which believe it or not, will make you feel less peckish.

- Apply coconut oil directly to your skin and it will leave you looking younger and fresher by moisturising and nurturing your body as well as acting as a sunscreen.

- And last but not least, coconut oil is great for your hair, shielding it from damage.

Courgettes

Courgettes are rich in dietary fibre, and have traces of copper, phosphorus, magnesium and vitamin A.

- They are a great vegetable to eat after you've been working out at the gym.

Dates

Dates are one of the oldest and loveliest food sources in the world.

- They're usually sweet and sticky when ripe and you can eat them for breakfast by adding them to cereals, snacking on them at any time of the day, or by putting them into cakes and biscuits.

- They're tasty when raw and are packed with minerals including iron, potassium, magnesium, copper, calcium and sulphur.

Eggs

Eggs are a great source of protein particularly if you separate the yolk from the white. This is because the white contains most of the good protein, together with vitamins B2, B6, D and B12 plus minerals such as iron, which is good for the blood.

Fish

Certain types of fish, specifically very oily fish such as salmon and mackerel, reduce fat build-up in the arteries and help to lower blood pressure.

- Try to look for products that are ethically sourced in a natural way as opposed to farmed.

Grapefruit

Grapefruits came about as a result of crossbreeding oranges and pomelos in the 18th century.

- They're high in Vitamin C, which supports our immune systems, as well as potassium, which is very good for the heart.

- Grapefruits contain something called pectin, a form of fibre that is soluble and has been shown to slow down the progression of atherosclerosis in pigs. It's an easy fruit to work with, but it can have a sour after taste.

Kiwi

Kiwi is a small fruit that has loads of magnesium and potassium in it, as well as serotonin, which is the wonderful stuff that boosts your memory and learning capacity, as well as helping to stabilise your appetite.

- Kiwis are yummy in cakes, tarts and fresh salads or as part of your breakfast.

- They're also a great alternative to crisps or sweets for young children as well as us adults.

Lettuce

Popular with the ancient Egyptians, high in Vitamin B and magnesium, you can eat lettuce raw or as an oil.

- It's well known for its anti-inflammatory benefits and is also said to help protect neuronal function in the brain, so encouraging memory retention.

- Plus, it's great for regulating our sleep patterns and is a marvellous antioxidant.

Mango

Mango is one of the world's favourite fruits. Gorgeously sweet and succulent, it can potentially protect against skin cancer, as well as help maintain the alkaline balance in our bodies due to the high vitamin C content. What's more, it's high in iron, good for your digestion and it's a natural skin cleanser.

Nectarines

This delicious fruit is rammed with vitamins C & A, niacin and folic acid. They also contain antioxidants that are thought to protect against arthritis, heart disease and other medical conditions including cancer. Nectarines are best eaten raw, and you benefit from most of their goodness that way, but, like many fruits, they also make tasty jams and jelly.

Olives

Olives contain monosaturate or healthy fat. These fatty acids also help to nourish and protect the skin from day-to-day wear and tear. In addition, they're a great source of iron and contribute to eye health. Black olives in particular can help prevent heart disease and have many cardiovascular benefits.

Pomegranates

This fruit is rich in fibre, protein, vitamin C and vitamin K.

It's loaded with important nutrients too. The seeds of the pomegranate are also bioactive.

Quinoa

Quinoa has become massively popular and can now be found quite easily on supermarket shelves. It's a gluten-free alternative to rice or pasta and it contains iron, magnesium, phosphorus and vitamin E as well as nine essential amino acids with many beneficial anti-oxidants for the body.

Radishes

Radishes are surprisingly rich in potassium and folic acid. They also contain traces of copper and vitamin B6 together with fibre. And because of their high levels of water retention, they're good for healthy moisturised skin.

Spinach

A member of the quinoa and beet family, spinach is excellent for regulating blood pressure, eye care and general wellbeing. It's low in fat and cholesterol and is rich in vitamins A, E, K, B6 and C. Additionally, it's highly beneficial for the cardiovascular system as well as maintaining good brain function.

Turmeric

This is a spice largely used in curry dishes, curcumin

being the main active ingredient. It has remarkable anti-inflammatory qualities, and by increasing the anti-oxidant capacity of the body, it protects us from free radicals. Other benefits include lowering the risk of brain and heart disease, and fighting the aging process.

Yam

Potatoes have become a staple food in modern society. But did you know that yams and sweet potatoes are a healthier alternative and are much better for your body? They're incredibly versatile, too, and go perfectly with other vegetables and meat.

Food for Thought

Due to changing legislation, it's now become more acceptable for food companies to use factory farmed and GM foods. However, you can still buy organic produce at farmers' markets. That way, you'll be eating better as well as supporting your local economy by keeping small independent shops and stores in business. Plus, you'll be doing your bit to decrease our carbon footprint and help society to maintain high standards in food production. Some supermarkets also stock organic or free-range products on their shelves so make sure you check labels thoroughly to ensure that what you're buying is healthy and nutritious.

CHAPTER TWELVE

Summary

The fashion industry can be a complex and exclusive beast. If you really want to be a model then you must identify your look and what you are most suited to. Be gentle, humble, respectful, gracious and never put anyone else down. Do your research, and be well prepared for castings and shoots. That way, photographers can do so much more with you and will enjoy the experience; which means they'll want to book you again.

There are all sorts of opportunities and careers available within the industry; make sure you explore your options thoroughly and decide what's best for you. Investigate courses, universities and independent organisations to find out which can help you to achieve your goal. Don't forget: the fashion industry is shaped by trends as well as wider political, social, economic, technological and environmental issues. There are however many brands within it that are dedicated to protecting the environment and championing diversity. It's important to grasp these influences so that you can understand how you will be perceived or where you might best fit. Decide your own success and never be defined by anyone else. You can achieve this quickly and easily by creating a goal book and being specific about where you really want to be in the future.

There are many misconceptions about models. Never feel afraid to use your profile to support and promote humanitarian causes. Just because you work in fashion doesn't mean you shouldn't care or need to hide your intelligence.

Industry Contacts

THE FOLLOWING is a concise guide to a selection of reputable names.

Useful Links for Models

The British Fashion Model Agents Association
www.associationofmodelagents.org
www.bfmaa.org

The International Model and Talent Association
www.imta.com

Useful Links for Creatives

Fashion Buyer and PR:

UAL London College of Fashion
www.arts.ac.uk

Open Study College
Parsons School of Design
Introduction to Fashion Buying
www.newschool.edu
www.openstudycollege.com

Public Relations:

Academy of Art University
info.art.edu
School of Fashion

Fashion Writer:

British Association of Journalists
www.bajunion.org.uk

Society of Professional Journalists
www.spj.org

Fashion Stylist:

British College of Styling
britishcollegeofprofessionalstyling.com

Domos Academy
www.landing.domusacademy.com

Make-up Artists:

Make-up Academy, The Royal College of Art
admissions@makeupacademy.co.uk
www.makeupacademy.co.uk

AOFM
www.aofmakeup.com

Photographers:

The Royal College of Art
www.rca.ac.uk

New York Film Academy
www.nyfa.edu

Fashion Designer:

Edinburgh College of Art
www.eca.ed.ac.uk

Central Saint Martins
www.arts.ac.uk/csm

Academy of Art
www.info.academyart.edu

Producer:

MET Film School
www.metfilmschool.ac.uk

Dub Spot
www.dubspot.com

Sales:

Reed
www.reed.co.uk

Bridge
www.getbridge.com

Press:

Press Association
www.pressassociation.com

Udemy
www.about.udemy.com

Other Useful Contacts:

British Fashion Council
www.britishfashioncouncil.co.uk

UK Fashion and Textile Association
www.ukft.org

Foreign Press Association
www.fpalondon.net

New York Fashion Week
mbfashionweek.com

London Fashion Week
www.londonfashionweek.co.uk

Paris Fashion Week
www.modeaparis.com/en

Milan Fashion Week
fashionweekonline.com/milan

Bibliography

Books

Church Gibson, Pamela., (2013), *Fashion and Celebrity Culture*, Berg.

Crane, D., (2012), *Fashion and Its Social Agendas: Class, Gender, and Identity in Clothing*, University of Chicago Press.

Hayward, M., Rublack, U., and Tiramani, J., (2015), *The First Book of Fashion: The Book of Clothes of Matthaeus and Veit Konrad Schwarz of Augsburg*, Bloomsbury.

Hirsch, G., (2015), *Gertie's New Fashion Sketchbook: Indispensable Figure Templates for Body-Positive Design*, Stewart, Tabori & Chang.

Kasier, Susan. B., (2014), *Fashion and Cultural Studies*, Edit Edition illustrated, Berg.

The Fashion Book – Mini Edition (2001), Phaidon Press.

Online Resources

Fashion United Global www.fashionunited.com/global-fashionindustry-statistics

'Breaking the Skinny White Mold: How Diversity in the Fashion Industry is slowly but surely changing', Grace Austin.
www.diversityjournal.com/9878-breaking-the-skinny-white-mold-how-diversity-inthe-fashion-industry-is-slowly-but-surely-changing

Collaboration for Health 2012: The Benefits of Regular Walking for Health, Wellbeing and the Environment, Christine Hancock Registered Charity
www.c3health.org

The Business of Fashion www.businessoffashion.com

Personal References:
Richard Biedul
Ioannis Koussertari
Joshua Kane
Kim Howells
Caryn Franklin

Endnotes

1   www.vogue.it/en/magazine/editor-s-blog/ 2011/04/
    april-19th
2   Breaking the Skinny White Mould: How Diversity in
    the Fashion Industry is slowly but surely changing,
    Grace Austin
    www.diversityjournal.com/9878-breaking-the-skinny-
    white-mold-howdiversity-in-the-fashion-industry-is-
    slowly-but-surely-changing
3   LVMH and Kering have drawn up a charter on working
    relations with fashion models and their well-being,
    September 6, 2017
    www.lvmh.com/news-documents/press-releases/
    lvmh-and-kering-have-drawn-up-a-charter-on-working-
    relations-with-fashion-models-and-their-well-being
4   Collaboration for Health 2012: The Benefits of regular
    walking for health, wellbeing and the environment,
    Christine Hancock Registered Charity www.c3health.
    org/ Christine Hancock

Photography Credits

THE IMAGE numbers stated below refer to the numerical sequence in which the images appear throughout the book.

Arved Colvin-Smith

arvedcolvin-smith.com

Images 28–29

Watch This Space Fashion Exhibition, Olumide Gallery

Photography	Arved Colvin-Smith
Photography assistant	Kai Cem Narin
Creative Director	Eunice Olumide
Fashion Director	Kim Howells
Styling assistants	Emi Papanikola, Donika Andreson, Femi Hurley-Scott
Digi tech	Sacha Phillips
Make-up	James O'Riley at Premier using MAC
Make-up assistant	Victoria Todd
Hair	Nick Irwin
Nails	Joanna Newbold
Editorial for	*Hunger* magazine

Dawn Marie Jones

Stoyanov and Jones

hello@stoyanovandjones.com

www.stoyanovandjones.com

Image 31

Photographer	Dawn Marie Jones
Model	Johanna Ristau
HMUA	Helen Leonard
Jewellery	Azarai

Images 32 33

Photographer	Dawn Marie Jones
Model	Craig McGinley
HMUA	Lien Vy
Stylist	Jo Ottaway

Image 37

Photos and Styling	Dawn Marie Jones
Model	Leili St Clair @ Nevs
MUA	Sally Bahri
Hair	Anton Alexander

Eunice Olumide

info@euniceolumide.com

www.euniceolumide.com

Images 45–54

Ioannis Koussertari

info@ioanniskoussertari.com

www.ioanniskoussertari.com

Images 17–20, 22

Photography   Ioannis Koussertari

Retouching   Alisa Nuanchan

BTS Talent

Maximilian Hetherington

mxhthrngtn@gmail.com

www.maximilianhetherington.com

Images 23–27, 30, 34–35

O.G. Studios

Morgan White

info@morganwhitephotography.co.uk

www.morganwhitephotography.co.uk

Image 39

Image 40–42

Stylist   Kim Howells

Hair   Amiee Robinson

Makeup   Mel Arter @ CLM

Models   Emma C @ IMG and Bara @ Union

Sorapol London

Sorapol Chawaphatnakul and Daniel Lismore
jackie@sorapol.co.uk

Images 1–7 s/s 15 Look book
Image 8 a/w 16 Look book
Images 9–12 a/w 15
Images 13–15 a/w 16
Image 16 s/s 16

William Pine

Lucy Siegle section images 43–44
Photography Will Pine
Clothing Katharine Hamnett